ICONS

SABRINA CARPENTER

BY KATHLEEN CONNORS

Enslow PUBLISHING

Please visit our website, www.enslow.com.
For a free color catalog of all our high-quality books, call toll free 1-800-398-2504 or fax 1-877-980-4454.

Library of Congress Cataloging-in-Publication Data

Names: Connors, Kathleen, author.
Title: Sabrina Carpenter / Kathleen Connors.
Description: Buffalo, New York : Enslow Publishing, 2026. | Series: Icons | Includes index.
Identifiers: LCCN 2025003306 (print) | LCCN 2025003307 (ebook) | ISBN 9781978544581 (library binding) | ISBN 9781978544574 (paperback) | ISBN 9781978544598 (ebook)
Subjects: LCSH: Carpenter, Sabrina--Juvenile literature. | Singers--United States--Juvenile literature. | LCGFT: Biographies.
Classification: LCC ML3930.C2633 C65 2026 (print) | LCC ML3930.C2633 (ebook) | DDC 782.42164092 [B]--dc23/eng/20250131
LC record available at https://lccn.loc.gov/2025003306
LC ebook record available at https://lccn.loc.gov/2025003307

Published in 2026 by
Enslow Publishing
2544 Clinton Street
Buffalo, NY 14224

Designer: Tanya Dellaccio Keeney
Editor: Kristen Rajczak Nelson

Photo credits: Cover, p. 5 Featureflash Photo Agency/Shutterstock.com; pp. 7, 9, 13, 15 WENN Rights Ltd/Alamy Images; p. 11 Photo 12/Alamy Images; p. 12 Tsuni/USA/Alamy Images; p. 16 ZUMA Press. Inc./Alamy Images; p. 17 The Photo Access/Alamy Images; p. 19 MediaPunch Inc/Alamy Images; pp. 20, 29 Sipa USA/Alamy Images; p. 21 AFF/Alamy Images; p. 23 Image Press Agency/Alamy Images; p. 25 Tom Rose/Alamy Images; p. 27 Everett Collection Inc/Alamy Images.

Printed in China

CPSIA compliance information: Batch #CSENS26: For further information contact Enslow Publishing, at 1-800-398-2504.

Contents

Words in the glossary appear in **bold** the first time they are used in the text.

A Big Year

In 2024, Sabrina Carpenter was everywhere! Her songs seemed to be playing all the time, she appeared on one of the biggest **tours** ever, and she even sang on *Saturday Night Live*. But Sabrina didn't just get started. She's been hard at work since childhood!

ICONIC!

Sabrina is only about 5 feet (1.5 m) tall.

3D
AUDIO

The Carpenters

Sabrina was born on May 11, 1999, in East Greenville, Pennsylvania. She lived with her parents, Elizabeth and David Carpenter. Sabrina has three older sisters, Cayla, Shannon, and Sarah.

ICONIC!

Sabrina sometimes works with her sisters. Sarah has sung with Sabrina, and Cayla has done Sabrina's hair for events.

David
Elizabeth
Sarah

Just A Kid

Sabrina started **performing** when she was a kid. Sabrina told *W Magazine* in 2024: "I can't even remember when I started singing and performing and **entertaining**, because I was really, really little." She began posting videos of herself singing on YouTube at age 9.

ICONIC!

Sabrina started out singing other artists' songs in her videos. Then, she started writing her own music!

Disney
Sofia the First
Once Upon A Princess
Disney
Disney Junior

Acting Success First

Sabrina started auditioning, or trying out, for TV shows and movies around age 11. She got small parts on *Law & Order: Special Victims Unit* and *Orange is the New Black*. She also appeared in the movie *Horns*.

ICONIC!

Sabrina was surprised by how serious her first acting ***roles*** *were. She thought she would do comedy, or shows and movies meant to make people laugh.*

Sabrina in Horns

Sabrina's big break in acting came when she was only 13. She landed the part of Maya Hart on the Disney Channel show *Girl Meets World.* As one of the main characters on the show, Sabrina was really in the spotlight!

Girl Meets World cast

ICONIC!

Before Sabrina got the part on Girl Meets World, *she signed a record deal with Disney's record label, Hollywood Records.*

First Albums

Girl Meets World came out in 2014. While Sabrina acted on the show, she was working on music too. Her first album, *Eyes Wide Open*, came out in 2015. Her second album, *EVOlution*, came out in 2016. The songs were fun to dance to!

ICONIC!

*Sabrina said in 2015 that there are a lot of "crazy ups and downs" when building a **career** in entertainment.*

In Two Acts

In 2018, Sabrina put out *Singular: Act I*. *Singular: Act II* came out the next year. These albums were considered two parts of one project. The albums started to really show off Sabrina's songwriting skills!

ICONIC!

Sabrina told Vogue that writing songs about her life has always been a way of "healing" herself and better understanding things that happened.

Making Movies

Girl Meets World ended in 2017. But Sabrina wasn't done with acting yet! She appeared in the movies *The Hate U Give* in 2018 and *Tall Girl* in 2019. She also starred in *Work It* and *Clouds* in 2020.

ICONIC!

Sabrina had to pretend to be a bad dancer in* Work It. *In truth, she had been dancing since childhood!

VOICE.

Broadway Bummer

In 2020, the COVID-19 **pandemic** shut down all Broadway shows. This included *Mean Girls*, the show Sabrina had prepared for months to star in. She only got to perform two shows before all Broadway theaters went dark.

ICONIC!

Sabrina has said that being on Broadway was a dream of hers.

Emailing Herself

Sabrina spent a lot of time writing by herself during the pandemic. Sometimes, she would write emails to herself, working through whatever her feelings were at the time. Some of this writing led to her 2022 album, *Emails I Can't Send*.

ICONIC!

Emails I Can't Send *was Sabrina's first album on a new label: Island Records.*

Time to Tour

Sabrina went on tour for *Emails I Can't Send*. She also appeared as the opening act on one of the biggest tours of all time: Taylor Swift's The Eras Tour. Sabrina performed at 25 stops in 2023 and 2024.

ICONIC!

On The Eras Tour, Sabrina didn't have dancers or sets. She had to put on a good show as just herself with her music!

"Espresso"

In 2024, Sabrina put out one of the biggest songs of the year: "Espresso." It was the first single off her album *Short n' Sweet* that came out in August 2024. *Short n' Sweet* hit number one on the *Billboard* Hot 200!

ICONIC!

In September 2024, Sabrina had three songs in the top five of the* Billboard *Hot 100—"Espresso," "Please, Please, Please," and "Taste."

In September 2024, Sabrina set out on her first **arena** tour. She performed sold-out shows across North America and then headed to Europe in March 2025. Sabrina has truly become an **icon** in the music world! What will she do next?

ICONIC!

In 2025, Sabrina won two Grammy Awards—which are honors in the music world—including best pop solo performance for "Espresso."

Timeline

1999	Sabrina is born May 11 in Pennsylvania.
2014-2017	She plays Maya Hart on *Girl Meets World*.
2015	*Eyes Wide Open* comes out.
2016	*EVOlution* comes out.
2018	*Singular: Act I* comes out.
2019	*Singular: Act II* comes out.
2020	She performs in two shows of *Mean Girls* on Broadway before the COVID-19 pandemic shuts down all Broadway theaters.
2022	*Emails I Can't Send* comes out.
2023-2024	Sabrina opens for Taylor Swift on The Eras Tour.
2024	*Short n' Sweet* comes out.
2025	Sabrina wins two Grammy Awards.

For More Information

BOOKS

Berne, Emma Carlson. *Olivia Rodrigo: All Access*. United States: Scholastic Inc., 2025.

Taylor, Susan Johnston. *Selena Gomez*. Mankato, MN: Apex Editions, 2025.

WEBSITE

Sabrina Carpenter
https://www.sabrinacarpenter.com/
Follow everything Sabrina is doing here.

Sabrina Carpenter – IMDb
https://www.imdb.com/name/nm4248775/
Keep up with all things Sabrina on IMDb.

Publisher's note to educators and parents: Our editors have carefully reviewed these websites to ensure that they are suitable for students. Many websites change frequently, however, and we cannot guarantee that a site's future contents will continue to meet our high standards of quality and educational value. Be advised that students should be closely supervised whenever they access the internet.

Glossary

arena: An enclosed area used for sports games and other entertainment.

career: A job someone does for a long time.

entertain: To do things that are interesting for people to watch or listen to.

icon: A person who is very successful and admired.

pandemic: A time when a disease, or sickness, spreads quickly and affects a large number of people in a place or throughout the world.

perform: To play music or sing.

role: The part a person plays.

tour: A trip to many places in order to play and sing music for people.

Index